# TOP SECRET

Written by:
Kirsten Hall

Illustrations by:
Rémy Simard

tangerine
press

# WELCOME!

Welcome to Top Secret—the journal designed to teach you all there is to know about secret codes and how to break them.

Inside, you will face thirteen top secret missions. As you will see, they start out pretty easy—but beware! They will get gradually more and more challenging.

Each mission that is completed will bring you that much closer to becoming A TOP SECRET AGENT.

## YOUR SECRET AGENT NAME:

# YOUR MISSION AGENDA

# MISSION:

### Learn to break codes written in reverse lettering

Task Requirements:
Intense Concentration

**1**

One way to write top secret information is to write it backwards—not just the words, but even the letters themselves!

## CAN YOU READ THE MESSAGE BELOW?

What's the biggest secret you've ever kept?

This way

This way

This way

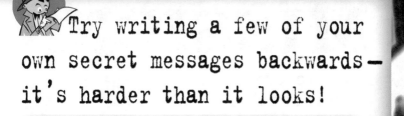

Try writing a few of your own secret messages backwards— it's harder than it looks!

1.

2.

3.

# MISSION: 2

## Learn to break codes in which numbers replace letters

**Task Requirements:**
An Eye for Reorganization

This code involves substituting numbers for letters. In the simplest version of this code, you switch each letter for its number in the alphabet. 1 will stand for A, 2 will stand for B, 3 will stand for C, and so forth.

| 1 | 2 | 3 | 4 | 5 | 6 | 7 | 8 | 9 | 10 | 11 | 12 | 13 | 14 | 15 |
|---|---|---|---|---|---|---|---|---|----|----|----|----|----|----|
| A | B | C | D | E | F | G | H | I | J  | K  | L  | M  | N  | O  |

| 16 | 17 | 18 | 19 | 20 | 21 | 22 | 23 | 24 | 25 | 26 |
|----|----|----|----|----|----|----|----|----|----|----|
| P  | Q  | R  | S  | T  | U  | V  | W  | X  | Y  | Z  |

Another option is to assign the numbers to the letters in any way you want to! Try it with these numbers.

| 1 | 2 | 3 | 4 | 5 | 6 | 7 | 8 | 9 | 10 |
|---|---|---|---|---|---|---|---|---|----|
| _ | _ | _ | _ | _ | _ | _ | _ | _ | _  |

| 11 | 12 | 13 | 14 | 15 | 16 | 17 | 18 |
|----|----|----|----|----|----|----|----|
| _  | _  | _  | _  | _  | _  | _  | _  |

| 19 | 20 | 21 | 22 | 23 | 24 | 25 | 26 |
|----|----|----|----|----|----|----|----|
| _  | _  | _  | _  | _  | _  | _  | _  |

# NOW TRY TO READ THE FOLLOWING NUMBER CODES:

23 8 15     11 14 5 23     14 21 13 2 5 18 19
3 15 21 12 4     2 5     19 15     13 21 3 8
6 21 14?

4 15     25 15 21     20 8 9 14 11
20 8 9 19     3 15 4 5     9 19
5 1 19 25     15 18     8 1 18 4?

ARE YOU READY TO CREATE YOUR
OWN NUMBER CODES?

# MISSION: 3

Learn to decipher
scrambled codes

Task Requirements:
An Eye for Reorganization

One way some code masters throw people off
is by scrambling words. For example,
instead of writing "boy," you can write
"oyb."

## CAN YOU UNSCRAMBLE
## THE FOLLOWING MESSAGE?

Deargni ascemrdbl agsesesm
can eb gouth!

Unscramble message here:

# NOW WRITE A COUPLE OF YOUR OWN CMAERSBDL ESAESGSM:

1.

2.

3.

Yeh!

Tswa'h Pu?

# MISSION:

## Learn to decode more scrambled messages

Task Requirements:
Same as Mission #3

By breaking up the scrambled words with dashes, you can be really confusing! Try to solve the following code by unscrambling. Remember that the dashes can break words where they shouldn't necessarily be broken!

Is-ht s-I a rl-e-lay -ifif-cut-ld eoc-d ot -ear-bk-!

### DECODE MESSAGE HERE

50-meter dash

ACM

START

Now, agent, it's your turn to write some of your own codes using both scrambles and dashes.

1.

2.

3.

# MISSION:

Learn to crack codes by reading every other letter.

After you've read all the first letters in every pair, go back and read the second letters to complete the message.

Task Requirements:
Strong Concentration

## TRY TO BREAK THE FOLLOWING CODE ON YOUR OWN:

RE ET AT DE ER VT EO RC
YR SA EC CK OT NH DI LS.

DID YOU FIGURE IT OUT?

Here's another for you:

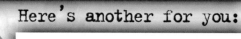

RC AA TL EE TF HR IO SM
CO ON DE ET OO NT AE SN.

## NOW TRY
## WRITING YOUR
## OWN!

# MISSION: 6

## Learn to break codes written in phonetic alphabet

Task Requirements:
Good Reference Skills

Sometimes, when people want to guarantee they are being understood correctly, they use a phonetic alphabet. For example, they might say something like, "Pizza"—"p" as in Peter, "i" as in Ida, etc.

Following is the phonetic alphabet that is used by the New York Police Department:

| | | | | | |
|---|---|---|---|---|---|
| A | Adam | J | John | S | Sam |
| B | Boy | K | King | T | Tom |
| C | Charlie | L | Lincoln | U | Union |
| D | David | M | Mary | V | Victor |
| E | Edward | N | Nora | W | William |
| F | Frank | O | Ocean | X | X-ray |
| G | George | P | Peter | Y | Young |
| H | Henry | Q | Queen | Z | Zebra |
| I | Ida | R | Robert | | |

# THERE ARE DIFFERENT WAYS YOU CAN USE THIS PHONETIC ALPHABET.

01: You can write a simple message substituting phonetic letters for their counterparts: John Union Sam Tom Lincoln Ida King Edward Tom Henry Ida Sam

02: You can make your message more complicated by using all lower case: lincoln ida king edward tom henry ida sam

03: Or you can break up the words and capitalize in the wrong places: Lin Coln Id A Kin Gedwa Rdt Omhe Nry Idas Am

04: And add random punctuation: Lin? Coln Id "A Kin" Gedwa. Rdt: Omhe/Nry Idas Am!

# NOW TRY TO DECODE THESE!

Willi Am hen Ryad Am To mda Vi Do Ce
Any Oun goce Anun ion To mhen ryi Dano Ra
king O Cean Fran kyo un goc ea Nuni Onrob
Ert Jo hnoce An Uni onro Be rt No Raad am
lin Co Lnsa Mocea n fra nkad Amrob ert?

## TRANSLATE IT HERE!

Da? Vido: cea nyo Un g  o  Cea 'n' uNi =on=
TO m.h.e.n.r. Y I D an o;r A K I  ng to
M\hen\r yed war dsa med W A R d???Ad Am Ro
be R "t" Ed WaR; dh Enr Yad AM Robe /r/ Tda
Vi D?

## TRANSLATE IT HERE!

Top notch work. You're doing an excellent job. All you need to do now is practice writing some of your own phonetic alphabet messages—then, it's off to the next mission!

Your message #1:

Your message #2:

Your message #3:

# MISSION:

## Learn to translate cryptograms

Task Requirements:
Strong Substitution Skills

Codes can be words that are switched around in order to confuse an outsider. Cryptograms, on the other hand, involve substituting one letter for another.

(This is a little like what you did in Mission #2, except that now you're substituting letters for letters—instead of numbers!)

Sometimes the switch is as easy as moving each letter up by one. For example, the letter "a" changes to "z," the letter "b" changes to "a," the letter "c" changes to "b," and so forth.

## TRY DECODING THE FOLLOWING CRYPTOGRAM:

Xibu't zpvs gbwpsjuf uijoh up fbu?

You're name is no longer Ben. Now you're Charlie!

18

What about if we switch the order of the code? Try switching each letter to the one that falls after it in the alphabet. "c" will now be "d," "b" will now be "c," and "z" will go up to "a."

**IS DECODING THE FOLLOWING CRYPTOGRAM HARDER OR EASIER THIS WAY?**

H vntkc ad rn gzoox he
H vdqd ehmzkkx zkknvdc sn . . .

Actually, I like the name Adam better!

TRY CREATING YOUR OWN
CRYPTOGRAPHIC ALPHABET!
AND DO IT IN INVISIBLE INK IF YOU
WANT IT TO BE SECRET!

| | | |
|---|---|---|
| A _____ | J _____ | S _____ |
| B _____ | K _____ | T _____ |
| C _____ | L _____ | U _____ |
| D _____ | M _____ | V _____ |
| E _____ | N _____ | W _____ |
| F _____ | O _____ | X _____ |
| G _____ | P _____ | Y _____ |
| H _____ | Q _____ | Z _____ |
| I _____ | R _____ | |

NOW I KNOW M? R, S, Ts!

Now try writing some secret messages
with your new crypto-alphabet!

1. _____

_____

_____

2. _____

_____

_____

3. _____

_____

_____

# MISSION: 8

Learn to read block codes

Task Requirements:
Strong Reorganizational Skills

A block code is one
that is written in a preset
number of spaces before it
shifts to the next line.

Thisi
showa
block
codel
ooks.

NOT
WRITER'S
BLOCK
AGAIN!

Think that's too easy? Here's how to make it harder. Write down the letters in the block, working your way from the top to the bottom of the first column. Then do the same for each of the other columns. Here's how it should look:

Tsaood/hamfce/inpak./selbc/ixelo

IF YOU WERE TO SEND THAT MESSAGE TO FRIENDS, WOULD THEY HAVE ANY IDEA WHAT YOU WERE SAYING? PROBABLY NOT! BUT YOU CAN SHARE THE CODE WITH THOSE YOU DO WANT TO KNOW THE MESSAGE. AS FOR THE REST OF THEM—

WHO CARES???

Auiieta/rfnshok/eigcab?/yntorr/odhdde

Dtyvtkbcg/ohoeieere/yiuwtsaen/onhhttstt/ukaaaoea?

Here's a real challenge.

```
3  9  5  1  18 / 15  14  19  12  4 /
   13  7  9  12  ! / 2  3  19  25 /
      9  15  18  8 / 14  4  5  1
```

# NOW WRITE YOUR OWN BLOCK CODE MESSAGES HERE:

1.

2.

3.

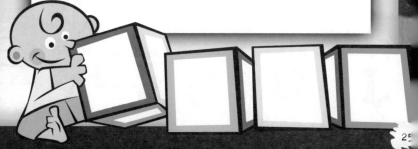

# MISSION:

## Learn Morse Code
### Task Requirements:
Ability to Read Symbols
for Letters

Long before telephones even existed, people
communicated by telegraph. A man by the name of
Samuel F. B. Morse invented a code for the telegraph
by tapping out different sounds. He converted different
letters into different combinations of short taps
(dots) and longer taps (dashes).

| | | |
|---|---|---|
| A .— | K —.— | U ..— |
| B —... | L .—.. | V ...— |
| C —.—. | M —— | W .—— |
| D —.. | N —. | X —..— |
| E . | O ——— | Y —.—— |
| F ..—. | P .——. | Z ——.. |
| G ——. | Q ——.— | |
| H .... | R .—. | |
| I .. | S ... | |
| J .——— | T — | |

# NUMBERS

| | |
|---|---|
| 0 | ----- |
| 1 | .---- |
| 2 | ..--- |
| 3 | ...-- |
| 4 | ....- |
| 5 | ..... |
| 6 | -.... |
| 7 | --... |
| 8 | ---.. |
| 9 | ----. |

# PUNCTUATION

| | |
|---|---|
| Period | .-.-.- |
| Comma | --..-- |
| Colon | ---... |
| Question mark | ..--.. |
| Apostrophe | .----. |
| Hyphen | -....- |
| Brackets | -.--.- |
| Quotation marks | .-..-. |

Morse was so ingenious that he even solved the problem of making mistakes. To let a listener know there was a mistake, Morse suggested tapping eight short sounds (dots) in a row.

# THERE ARE MANY WAYS YOU CAN USE MORSE CODE

**Even without a telegraph! How about tapping on a drum?**

Your assignment is to read the following
messages written in Morse Code:

--/./.-/ --/. .-/- -/ .... /. .--/ .-/-/./.-.

.. -./---/. .-/-././-/../-. .-.-.-

_____

_____

-../--- -.--/---/..- .-/.-/-/ -/--- ..../.-/-./.--.

---/..-/- .-/...-/-/././-. .../-.-./..../---/---/.-.. ..--..

_____

_____

Hi! Hi!

AS A TOP SECRET AGENT, YOU WILL
BE EXPECTED TO KNOW HOW TO
WRITE YOUR OWN MESSAGES IN
MORSE CODE, AS WELL.

Write a few Top Secret messages here:

1. _____

_____

_____

2. _____

_____

_____

_____

# MISSION: 10

Learn to break pigpen codes

Task Requirements:
Same as for Mission #9

## TWO GRIDS

| AB | CD | EF |
|----|----|----|
| GH | IJ | KL |
| MN | OP | QR |

ST

UV    WX

YZ

Agent, your next mission will take place in the pigpen. (Well, not really—but "pigpen" is the name for this code!)

In order to write in pigpen code, you'll need to refer to these two grids.

30

Each letter is represented by its place in the pigpen. If it's the first letter in the "box," you just draw the shape of the box that's around it. If it's the second letter in the box, draw the shape and then add a dot to the middle.

## FOR EXAMPLE:

A = ⌐|

B = ●|

C = ⊔

X = <●

Y = ⋀

Z = >●

YOUR MISSION IS TO
TRANSLATE AND THEN ANSWER
THE FOLLOWING QUESTIONS
WRITTEN IN PIGPEN CODE:

# THIS MISSION HAS ALMOST BEEN COMPLETED.

Now write some of your own **pigpen** messages, to show you've really mastered the code.

1. _____

_____

_____

2. _____

_____

_____

# MISSION:

## Learn to read codes in outside sources

Task Requirements: Skill with Numbers

For starters, you'll need to make sure that both you and the person with whom you plan on sharing the code have copies of a piece of writing that is exactly the same. It can be a newspaper article, a page from a favorite book—even an old science report! The content is not important, since it will be used only as a source for letters and words.

## THE WAY THIS CODE WORKS SEEMS COMPLICATED, BUT, WITH YOUR SKILLS, YOU'RE BOUND TO GET THE HANG OF IT QUICKLY.

1. First, figure out what you want your message to be, and write it down.

2. Now, look at the piece of writing you've chosen. (Try to find a piece that has all of the letters of the alphabet!)

3. Find the first letter of your message. (What paragraph is it in? What number word is it in the paragraph? What number letter is it in the word?). A letter that falls in the third paragraph will start with the number 3. If it falls in the tenth word in that paragraph, you'll need to write: 3.10. And, if it's the fifth letter in that word, your code for the letter will be: 3.10.5.

# USE THE FOLLOWING STORY ABOUT THE SKYTALE FOR REFERENCE WHEN ANSWERING THE QUESTIONS AND SOLVING THE CODES ON THE NEXT PAGE.

Secret messages are nothing new to the people of Greece. Over 1,600 years ago, in the fifth century, the Spartans invented a secret message device called the "skytale." The skytale was a simple creation, but it worked brilliantly.

Back then, most people sent notes to one another by messenger. The skytale was created in order to ensure that a message didn't fall into the wrong hands along the way.

First, the writer would take a thin strip of paper and wind it diagonally around a cylinder (like a tube).

Then the writer would write the secret message. So, the note would not be written along the length of the paper like ours are today—instead, it followed the length of the cylinder! When it was unwound, the note could not be read. It would look just like a bunch of random, jumbled letters.

Obviously, it was important for the recipient of the message to know what to do—to wind the note back around another, identical cylinder. That would be the only way for the letters of the message to reappear in their correct order.

# READY TO DECIPHER YOUR MESSAGE, AGENT?

Remember, the first number stands for the paragraph number, the second number stands for the word number within that paragraph, and the third number stands for the letter number within the word.

4,8.6  1.4.2  2.3.2  5.15.1
4.3.1  3.4.2  1.1.4  1.28.2

Try writing your own secret message here:

_____

_____

_____

_____

# MISSION:

## Learn the Navajo phonetic alphabet

Task Requirements: Aptitude for Foreign Languages

During World War II, the American military was desperate for a secret language with which to communicate—and it needed to be one that no other nation would be able to understand. A man by the name of Philio Johnston suggested using a code based on the language of the Navajo people. The plan was approved, and just a short time later the newly trained Navajos became known as "Code Talkers." They were some of the most succesful code-users in all of history!

On the following two pages is the alphabet used by the Code Talkers of WWII. As you'll notice, some letters were represented by multiple words.

July 7, 1943

Private First Class Preston Toledo (left) and Private First Class Frank Toledo, cousins and Navajos, in the South Pacific relaying orders over a radio in their native tongue.

Photo courtesy of: U.S. MARINE CORPS

NAVAJO VOCABULARY

COPY NUMBER_____

| ALPHABET | NAVAJO WORD | LITERAL TRANSLATION |
|---|---|---|
| A | WOL-LA-CHEE | ANT |
| A | BEL-LA-SANA | APPLE |
| A | TSE-NILL | AXE |
| B | NA-HASH-CHID | BADGER |
| B | SHUSH | BEAR |
| B | TOISH-JEH | BARREL |
| C | MOASI | CAT |
| C | TLA-GIN | COAL |
| C | BA-GOSHI | COW |
| D | BE | DEER |
| D | CHINDI | DEVIL |
| D | LHA-CHA-EH | DOG |
| E | AH-JAH | EAR |
| E | DZEH | ELK |
| E | AH-NAH | EYE |
| F | CHUO | FIR |
| F | TSA-E-DONIN-EE | FLY |
| F | MA-E | FOX |
| G | AH-TAD | GIRL |
| G | KLIZZIE | GOAT |
| G | JEHA | GUM |
| H | TSE-GAH | HAIR |
| H | CHA | HAT |
| H | LIN | HORSE |
| I | TKIN | ICE |
| I | YEH-HES | ITCH |
| I | A-CHI | INTESTINE |
| J | TKELE-CHO-G | JACKASS |
| J | AH-YA-TSINNE | JAW |
| J | YIL-DOI | JERK |
| K | JAD-HO-LONI | KETTLE |
| K | BA-AH-NE-DI-TININ | KEY |
| K | KLIZZIE-YAZZIE | KID |
| L | DIBEH-YAZZIE | LAMB |
| L | AH-JAD | LEG |
| L | NASH-DOIE-TSO | LION |

7 Sept 44

COPY NUMBER_____

| ALPHABET | NAVAJO WORD | LITERAL TRANSLATION |
|---|---|---|
| M | TSIN-TLITI | MATCH |
| M | BE-TAS-TNI | MIRROR |
| M | NA-AS-TSO-SI | MOUSE |
| N | TSAH | NEEDLE |
| N | A-CHIN | NOSE |
| O | A-KHA | OIL |
| O | TLO-CHIN | ONION |
| O | NE-AHS-JAH | OWL |
| P | CLA-GI-AIH | PANT |
| P | BI-SO-DIH | PIG |
| P | NE-ZHONI | PRETTY |
| Q | CA-YEILTH | QUIVER |
| R | GAH | RABBIT |
| R | DAH-NES-TSA | RAM |
| R | AH-LOSZ | RICE |
| S | DIBEH | SHEEP |
| S | KLESH | SNAKE |
| T | D-AH | TEA |
| T | A-WOH | TOOTH |
| T | THAN-ZIE | TURKEY |
| U | SHI-DA | UNCLE |
| U | NO-DA-IH | UTE |
| V | A-KEH-DI-GLINI | VICTOR |
| W | GLOE-IH | WEASEL |
| X | AL-NA-AS-DZOH | CROSS |
| Y | TSAH-AS-ZIH | YUCCA |
| Z | BESH-DO-TLIZ | ZINC |

July 7, 1943

Corporal Lloyd
Oliver, a Navajo,
operates a radio
in the South
Pacific.  Cpl.
Oliver is also a
highly regarded
scout.

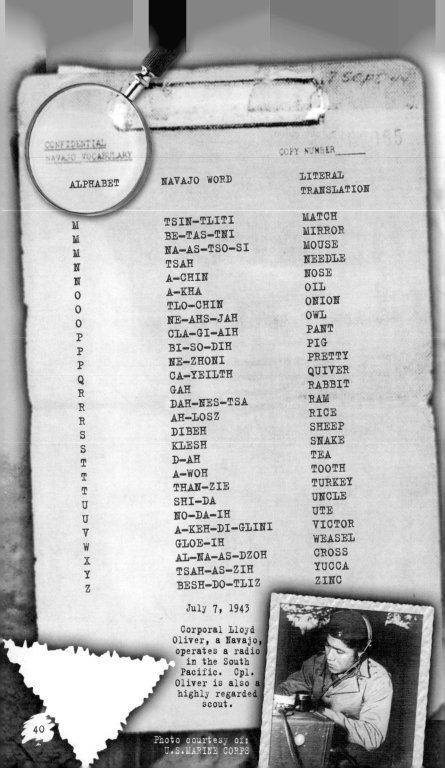

Photo courtesy of:
U.S. MARINE CORPS

40

# USING THE NAVAJO ALPHABET, TRY TO BREAK THE FOLLOWING CODE:

D-AH CHA DZEH / WOL-LA-CHEE BE-TAS-TNI

AH-NAH GAH A-CHI MOASI BEL-LA-SANA

A-CHIN KLESH / GLOE-IH AH-NAH GAH DZEH /

AH-JAD SHI-DA BA-GOSHI JAD-HO-LONI

TSAH-AS-ZIH / D-AH TLO-CHIN / CHA WOL-

LA-CHEE A-KEH-DI-GLINI AH-NAH / THAN-

ZIE LIN AH-NAH / LIN DZEH NASH-DOIE-

TSO BI-SO-DIH / TLO-CHIN CHUO / THAN-

ZIE LIN AH-NAH / TSAH BEL-LA-SANA

A-KEH-DI-GLINI WOL-LA-CHEE TKELE-CHO-G

TLO-CHIN DIBEH !

DO YOU AGREE?

## HERE ARE A FEW MORE CODES USING THE NAVAJO ALPHABET FOR YOU TO BREAK:

A-WOH CHA DZEH / YIL-DOI WOL-LA-CHEE
BI-SO-DIH BEL-LA-SANA TSAH AH-JAH KLESH
DZEH / NO-DA-IH DIBEH AH-JAH BE / WOL-
LA-CHEE / BA-GOSHI TLO-CHIN CHINDI AH-
NAH / MOASI BE-LA-SANA DIBEH-YAZZIE
AH-JAD AH-NAH LHA-CHA-EH / A-WOH CHA
DZEH / NE-ZHONI SHI-DA GAH CLA-GI-AIH
DIBEH-YAZZIE AH-JAH / MOASI A-KHA BE
DZEH .

YEH-HES A-WOH / GLOE-IH
BEL-LA-SANA KLESH /
WOL-LA-CHEE / BA-GOSHI TKIN
BI-SO-DIH TSE-GAH AH-NAH
DAH-NES-TSA / MOASI TLO-CHIN
CHINDI DZEH.

Write some of your own messages using the
Navajo Code Talkers' dictionary here:

1. _____

_____

_____

2. _____

_____

_____

3. _____

_____

_____

# MISSION:

**13**

Learn to communicate
in outer space!

Task Requirements:
An Ingenius Mind

SCIENTISTS HAVE LONG
WONDERED WHETHER OR NOT
THERE IS ANY OTHER FORM
OF INTELLIGENT LIFE
IN THE UNIVERSE.

IN FACT, SOME SCIENTISTS
SPEND THEIR TIME SENDING
SIGNALS INTO OUTER SPACE
IN HOPES OF GETTING A
RESPONSE. THE SIGNALS
ARE SENT IN THE FORM OF
LASER LIGHTS THAT FORM
DIFFERENT SHAPES.

The challenge we face when sending messages into outer space is that, even if there ARE different forms of life out there, we realize they won't understand our languages. So, we can't use words! Instead, the signals that are sent are shapes and symbols that spell out basic mathematical principles.

Our hope is that somewhere out there another form of intelligent life will receive the binary code, figure out its meaning, and send a similar message back in response.

We send one message several times over and over again, and then switch to the next. A simplified example of what one message might say is:

$$1 + 1 = 2$$

This message might be followed by another message which says:

$$2 + 2 = 4$$

WORKING WITH BINARY CODES IS A VERY
COMPLICATED TASK—EVEN FOR THE MOST
SKILLED TOP SECRET AGENTS. HOWEVER,
YOU CAN ACCOMPLISH THE SAME THING
THAT THE NASA SCIENTISTS DO—BY USING
SYMBOLS IN PLACE OF LETTERS IN ORDER
TO COMMUNICATE SIMPLE CONCEPTS.

FOR EXAMPLE:

CAN YOU GUESS WHAT THE CIRCLE
REPRESENTS IN THESE CODES?

# CODE 1

# CODE 2

47

MAKE UP
SOME OF
YOUR
OWN
CODES
HERE!

# FOR YOUR EYES ONLY

The following are the answers to the secret coded messages with which you've been challenged—not that you need them, of course!

## PAGE 4
What's the biggest secret you've ever kept?

## PAGE 7
Who knew numbers could be so much fun?

## PAGE 7
Do you think this code is easy or hard?

## PAGE 8
Reading scrambled messages can be tough!

## PAGE 10
This is a really difficult code to break!

## PAGE 12
Read every second letter to crack this.

## PAGE 13
Rate this code on a scale from one to ten.

## PAGE 14
Pretty neat, huh?

## PAGE 15
These are getting tough!

## PAGE 16
What do you think of your journal so far?

## PAGE 16
Do you think these are hard?

## PAGE 18
What's your favorite thing to eat?

## PAGE 19
I would be so happy if I were finally allowed to ...

## PAGE 22
This is how a block code looks.

**PAGE 23**
This is an example of a
block code.

**PAGE 24**
Are you finding this code
hard to break?

**PAGE 24**
Do you think you have what
it takes to be a secret
agent?

**PAGE 24**
Combining codes is really
hard!

**PAGE 26**
Morse code is fun.

**PAGE 27**
Even geniuses make mistakes?

**PAGE 27**
Sorry!

**PAGE 28**
Meet me at the water
fountain.

**PAGE 28**
Do you want to hang out
after school?

**PAGE 29**

So you better start practicing.

**PAGE 32**

Who would you never allow to read your journal?

**PAGE 32**

Is there anyone you would let read your journal?

**PAGE 33**

Great work!

**PAGE 37**

Good work!

**PAGE 41**

The Americans were lucky to have the help of the Navajos!

**PAGE 42**

The Japanese used a code called the Purple Code.

**PAGE 42**

It was a cipher code.

**PAGE 43**

Good work!

PAGE 46
$$2 + 2 = 4$$

PAGE 46
$$3 + 3 = 6$$

PAGE 46
$$2 - 1 = 1$$

PAGE 46
$$4 - 1 = 3$$

# CON-GRATU-LA-TIONS!

# TOP SECRET
## agent certificate

**Name:** _____

**Date:** _____

**Password:** _____